WHAT HAPPENS WHEN YOU
GET WHAT YOU WANT?

Success and the Challenge of Choice

Rick Eigenbrod, Ph.D.

Candescence Media
HALF MOON BAY, CALIFORNIA

eigenbrod@candescencemedia.com
www.CandescenceMedia.com

Ordering Information:
Quantity sales. Special discounts are available on quantity purchases by corporations, associations, and others. For details, contact the "Special Sales Department" at the address above.

What Happens When You Get What You Want?/ Frederick A. Eigenbrod. -- 1st ed.
ISBN 978-0-9900219-3-3

Contents

Acknowledgements 5

Preface: At the end of the trail 7

1: Agony of victory? In the land of plenty? 11

2: Well, everybody knows that! 15

3: Real problems in a strange place 19

4: Happily-ever-after? 23

5: A Grand Narrative of $uccess 27

6: The drug of choice 33

7: Suffer the children? 39

8: "What are you going to do?" 43

9: The chance to make a choice 47

10: The hero's journey, and ours 51

11: Is that all there is? 55

12: Making choices, Searching for meaning 59

13: Inklings of a new reality 63

14: On my blindness 67

15: The question that isn't asked 71

16: Becoming your own narrator 75

17: Making our own choices 79

18: Living freely in spaciousness 83

19: What's next? 89

Rick Eigenbrod, Ph.D. 91

Acknowledgements

I'd like to thank Kermit the Frog and all the generous people who have shared their experience, insights and inspiration when finding the Rainbow Connection.

Thanks go to every CEO, client and interviewee who talked honestly about what happened when they got what they wanted. They deepened the knowledge and added to the wisdom that make up these pages. In particular, Wes Bilson who started me on this curious journey, and Ken Saxon and Tom Bird who so bravely and impactfully leaned into the challenge of choice and demonstrated the possibility and power of exploring deeply personal territory to the benefit of others. My friend, Ray Rizzo, early on, offered me one expression of his organizing intention, to be generous, by volunteering to be my "lab rat".

Turning a talker into a writer isn't easy and it took the combined and additive talents of Clark Malcolm, Paul Wright and Dick Holm to get me there; and Linda Alvarez and her ace team at Candescence Media to transform manuscript into book. Tammy Sicard, Doug Bouey and Walt Sutton helped keep me going with everything from: "Don't lose faith, this is important" to "Yeah, writing is hard now shut up and do some."

I don't know if other writers have friends like Pat Murray and Jill Janov but can't imagine how they could write five sentences without these "pen-pals". I am forever in their debt and glad of it.

Is there anything more satisfying than becoming your children's student? My son Ian taught me, over and over, what clear writing looked like and when I just couldn't deliver, he did. My daughter, Megan, cracked my early narrow mindedness, challenging my belief that the emptiness accompanying gain and victory was a malady suffered only by "rich whiners." She helped open my eyes to the universality of the hazards of *having*.

There has not been one day, since I first stepped into the question that became this book, that my wife, Vicki, didn't make a contribution. Typing and thinking, cajoling and critiquing, encouraging and enduring, salving and celebrating; she always provided her highest and best contribution— Vicki. Life and writing are too hard to go through alone. Gratefully, I didn't.

At the end of the trail

Y ou'd think I would have known better.

After all that I've learned about what happens when I get what I want, and after all that I've heard from others about what happened when they got what they wanted, you'd think that I wouldn't have been surprised—staggered, even—by what happened when I finished my 500-mile, 35-day hike along the Camino de Santiago trail in Spain, at the age of 71.

The trip began long before I took my first step on the Camino. For the better part of a year I trained up and thinned down. I turned into an REI rat, examining all kinds of cool equipment and asking questions about this fabric and that gadget. I got more and more hyped up, sensing far in advance the exhilaration I'd feel when I completed my journey, when I'd be standing in the sun in front of the Cathedral of Santiago de Compostela among my fellow pilgrims and admiring townspeople. I knew that I would be filled with pride, accomplishment, and relief—and that, like St. James, from way up there on his pedestal, I would have an unbounded view of the landscape unfolding to infinity.

The real story? In the last days of walking there was cold, mud, mist, spit-slick footing, and fatigue rooted in daily effort and deepening depletion. When at last I arrived, there were few people on the streets and those that were moved with heads down, eyes focused one step ahead, like me. The Plaza was almost as empty as I was feeling. As I stood there looking up at the graven image of St. James, I realized, with sudden, fierce clarity, that I had taken my last step on the Camino. My next step would take me off it. I would walk out of life as I had known it.

While I was experiencing the reward of completing the journey, I was also feeling great losses. The loss of my place in a web of relationships and of my name, "Peregrino." The loss of rhythms and routines and a clarity of purpose. The loss of a destination and a glorious goal. I had ended out on unsettled ground. I had lost my place in the story.

Ralph Waldo Emerson wrote that "the reward of a thing well done is to have done it." Well, I had done a thing well but the "reward" I was feeling included a serious letdown, an emptiness that I wasn't prepared for.

But I should have known better. I shouldn't have been the least bit surprised.

As a clinical psychologist turned organizational psychologist, I've come to understand the seeming paradox of what happens when we get what we want. I've learned firsthand the meaning of Oscar Wilde's observation that "there are only two tragedies in life: one is not getting what one wants, and the other is getting it."

I've talked to people returning from the Peace Corps, kids graduating from college, people who got the big job, the big check, won the girl, the championship, the captaincy, finished the first marathon, the doctorate. The pattern was always the same. They all assumed that the process of achieving a goal would be hard but that, once achieved, living with it would be easy. Over and over their experiences have shown me that the big story of happily-ever-after isn't the whole story. Not even close.

I wrote this book to start the conversation we are *not* having, a conversation about the real story of what happens when dreams come true. I want to help people see that the results of getting what they want are natural, predictable, and developmental. I want to show them that not understanding what really happens when they get what they want undermines their readiness for the reality and the impact of success and their ability to benefit from all that success offers.

Knowing the real story won't protect you from the difficulties and challenges that come with acquisition and gain and "success," but it may insulate you from the corrosive doubt that something is wrong with how you got it or how fast you got there. I want to quell your suspicion that you failed at success, and I want you to understand that success is just as disruptive as failure and, unlike failure, that it comes without sympathy.

I need to remind myself of these things, too. Before my Camino trip, I had conjured up an illusion. Technically it's called a focusing illusion—a picture that draws the power to compel from what it leaves out. After my trip, after I was back home recovering—physically and emotionally—the illusion faded. I slowly regained my recognition that the end of a trip is where the real journey begins. It's all part of the timeless quest that Joseph Campbell reminds us is locally unique but universally the same.

The Camino experience is a fractal, a repetitive pattern of striving and arriving that cycles through our lives again and again. We move through that changing landscape many times. The journey ends and the call to a new one begins. Which journey? The one you choose, of course.

CHAPTER 1

Agony of victory?
In the land of plenty?

If there ever were a subject for a book that didn't need to be, "getting what you want" would certainly seem to qualify. How much can you say about the topic? To begin with, the question answers itself.

Question: "What happens when you get what you want?"

Answer: "You get what you want."

No prologue, no epilogue, and nothing in between needed. So just hold the words and spare the trees.

If you were to walk into a bookstore, you'd be hard pressed to find a section on "having what you want." Considering all the self-help manuals and spiritual guides that publishers crank out year after year, and seeing bookstore shelves stocked with advice on *getting* everything from lighter soufflés to tighter buns, you'd think there might be just a few words about *having*. Wrong—don't bother looking. It's not there.

Why would publishers bother with a question with such a self-evident answer? Everyone knows that when you get what you want, you enjoy it and you feel happier than before you got it. And, as an added bonus, you also feel more satisfied and contented, more safe and secure. By definition, you also feel more successful, since to succeed means to acquire or achieve what you want.

And, once you get whatever it is you want, there's always something else to want: more, and then more. This kind of never-ending need for more is cultivated in early childhood. (I'm reminded of a *New Yorker* cartoon where a young boy, surrounded by a raft of unwrapped Christmas presents and looking bewildered, asks his parents, "When is it time to want more?") Whatever your age, so it seems, you can never have enough of what you want—or already have plenty of. But that's all right because there's general agreement that getting what you want makes you happy and always gets you more. And when you get more, the benefits pile up in a self-generating, exponential, almost magical way. Happy plus more happy equals very happy. Very happy plus more happy equals wildly happy.

I know that's what I've been led to believe should happen when I'm successful at getting what I want. Now I know better, but that doesn't mean I can't still be seduced by the seeming promises of success. It doesn't mean that I don't still look hopefully ahead to what is *supposed* to happen at, say, the end of a 500-mile hike.

But enough about me.

What are your bedrock beliefs about success? Have you ever given careful thought to what happened when you got what you wanted?

Now, back to me.

I can't remember ever asking myself such questions in school and my early professional life. I just charged ahead, imagining what "getting" would be like before I got whatever it was that I wanted. I shaped compelling, hopeful stories that I could draw on, particularly when I needed to reassure or motivate myself to keep plugging away. I relied on little, private vignettes that served as great pep talks whenever my interest or enthusiasm started to drain away into doubt, disinterest, or just plain laziness.

I'm not alone when it comes to fantasizing about getting what I want. From what I've been able to gather, it's something we all do to greater or lesser degrees. For every goal we set, there's an accompanying picture of what will be ours, how we will feel, what we will do, how others will see us.

I was living in this looped scenario of my own making while working in Silicon Valley at the time it was turning into the real magic kingdom. Fields that just a few years before were pushing up almonds and cherry trees were sprouting companies and bazillionaires. There were plenty of places where there was no millionaire next door. The millionaire couldn't afford it.

Working in Silicon Valley in the 80s and 90s was like living in a petri dish of success, a place that was growing its own culture and ecosystem for entrepreneurial innovation. It had—and still has—a great location, a world-class university, smart people, youth, and an acceptance of eccentricity and different thinking. Great ideas, hard work, good luck—everything came together. It seemed that anyone could achieve anything on a grand scale. (Some called this the "democratization of success.") And in this pursuit of more and more success, we didn't stop to look at the impact. We just kept going for more.

It seemed to be working fine for a lot of people, and I was glad to be a part of it in my own way: consulting, listening, observing, asking, rubbing elbows. And then, in the mid and late 90s, I began to see the side of success that nobody was really talking about.

In what shouldn't have been to my surprise, I was finding myself being asked to help with what one person called "the agony of victory."

CHAPTER 2

Well, everybody knows that!

B ut, back to the question at hand. If "what happens when you get what you want?" isn't worth asking because we think we already know the answer, let's try another: How do we know we know? Where does this certainty of the rewards of success come from?

Well, we just know. We know because "everyone" told us so. We learn pretty quickly that life is about closing the gap between what we want and what we have. We're told over and over by parents, teachers, marketers, and the media that we should be after something and that we'll be measured by how quickly we get it, by how effectively we mine the gap between the current and desired situation. For every gap we discover, invent, or accept, we know what will happen when we close it: we will be happy with our achievement and with ourselves. Oh, and also handsomely rewarded with usual currency: stuff and status.

We hear stories that reinforce this from early childhood. Think about how most fairy tales end, reassuring us that happily-ever-after is the norm. Ride off into the sunset and fade to black. We're not invited to think much more about it. And we don't. Kids become coauthors of happily-ever-after by *not* asking: "Did Bambi survive the hunting season?" or "How did Snow White's marriage to the prince work out?" Leave well enough alone, children. If you don't bring it up, we won't either.

In his musical "Into the Woods," Stephen Sondheim ventures past the apparently happy ending. He invites us to consider the "what-happened-next" question by presenting familiar fairy-tale characters—including Jack, Little Red Riding Hood, Rapunzel, and Cinderella—at the point where we usually leave them. He forces us to go beyond the ending by having happily-ever-after come at the end of Act I, not Act III. Sondheim's subversive message: We don't go into the woods to seek what we want. We go there after we have it. Only then do we find what really happens after happily-ever-after.

Sondheim aside, you'd think we would be more prepared for the reality of what comes next, and not so ready to embrace the illusion. But who can blame us? Heading into the woods can be a scary venture, a trip into the unknowable. Who wants that?

We haven't changed our expectations of what happens when we get what we want since we were kids. Even in the face of experience, even though we know better, we're still looking for a Disney Channel ending. Like fairy tales, the movies we like tend to end right after some kind of triumph or epiphany or resolution, a magical moment that leaves us feeling uplifted or hopeful as we leave the theater. (European movies? Not so much.)

In "Rainbow Connection," Kermit the Frog, ever the voice of wisdom, sings about such self-deception: "Why are there so many songs about rainbows and what's on the other side? Rainbows are visions. They're only illusions." He asks this even as he hopes that someday "the lovers, the dreamers, and me, who said that every wish would be heard and answered," will find the Rainbow Connection.

All of us, more or less, count on over-the rainbow strategies, making when-then deals with ourselves throughout our lives. "When I get married, then I'll settle down and be happy." "When I get that sports car, then I'll feel freer." "When I get my degree, then the world will open up to me." "When I get past this project, then things will slow down and get easier."

You probably have one of these deals going on with yourself right now. See if you can put it into words, beginning with the conditional clause ("When I get...") and ending with the payoff ("then I will..."). When did you make that deal? What would it take for you to back out of it?

CHAPTER 3

Real problems in a strange place

W hat would be your reaction if you were told that achieving your goal would be far more challenging and disruptive than anything you ran into trying to get it? Exactly. People don't want to hear such things. They don't want to know. They need to believe the story of what will happen because they have so much riding on it. And they don't want anyone to dis their myth.

That was how it had been for Wes. Nobody, including himself, had ever dissed his quest for success, and what he was certain it would bring. That was why he was so stunned by what happened when he got what he wanted. And that was why he called me and later ran this notice in the Wall Street Journal:

SOLD MY BUSINESS

"I thought I had prepared myself for the changes that come with lots of cash and the loss of position, but I'm still uncertain and depressed. I can't exactly find a new rhythm to my

daily life. I'm forming a group of "retired" execs. If you are in a similar position and interested, reply to..."

Wes is one of those natural-born businesspeople who sees opportunities about every five minutes and who knows how to make things happen, like starting and selling a business. He'd done it before, selling another large company in a completely different industry, but selling his latest venture had left him deflated. After getting what he wanted, he was bummed—and he was bummed about being bummed. Not a patient guy, he wanted to figure a way out of this strange place.

Here he was—having grown a business like it was on steroids and having received an offer that his partners and investors couldn't pass up—making an early exit, his plan for a "liquidity event" realized much sooner than anyone had anticipated. And then he found out that he wasn't prepared for it. He had gotten what he wanted, but after the blur of lawyers, bankers, accountants, consultants, assorted rich guys, and champagne, he wasn't where he wanted to be.

Not one to panic, he figured this was just some kind of decompression period he needed to go through. Maybe he was suffering from a case of the bends brought on by coming up too fast from the high-pressure depths of where he'd been. But as the days and weeks passed, and as his uneasiness turned to real suffering, he felt there was nowhere to go and no one to talk to.

He imagined calling a doctor's office: "Hello. I'd like to make an appointment."

"OK. What are your symptoms?"

"I'm depressed, kind of lost. I'm even having trouble fig-
uring out what time to get up in the morning or what to do
when I do."

"How long has this been going on?"

"Since I sold my company."

"Excuse me?"

"I recently sold a company I owned and now I can do
whatever I want because I made lots of money."

"So you have tons of time, buckets of money, all the
freedom in the world and you want the doctor to help you
with this problem?"

"Yes, that's it."

"Sorry. We help people with real problems."

CHAPTER 4

Happily-ever-after?

So Wes called me instead, out of the blue. I had no idea what to make of him; I was too surrounded by the success of Silicon Valley. I didn't know what to do about the problem. More telling is that I didn't know how to think about it. I didn't know jack about *being* there. What I knew best was *trying to get there*. But, full of ignorance and confidence (and curiosity), I agreed to have the first of what would become many conversations with him.

I also started talking with other people. I put the word out that I wanted to talk about individuals' experiences with success. In return I would keep them informed about what I was hearing and learning and thinking. Not only were people— including professionals, students, recent grads, entrepreneurs, and a new bride—willing to talk to me, they were eager to. I asked for an hour and often got two or three, during which they answered three questions: What has been your experience? What has it bought you? What has it cost you? When we stopped, *they* thanked *me*!

At one point, Wes decided to see if there were others out there who were going through the same thing he was, so he ran the *Wall Street Journal* notice noted earlier.

To his surprise, over two dozen people responded. After meeting most of them personally, Wes decided to gather a group at his home. He invited about a dozen of them. He also invited me. The purpose: an honest chat about what happens when you get what you want. You should have been there. It was a revelation, an inside look at what we never consider.

At their initial gathering, and at subsequent sessions, I heard stories that blew apart suppositions about getting what we want. And, as I had time to consider what I was witnessing, I saw that what applies to rich older guys also applies to people of lesser means and younger ages. It's just a matter of degree, a difference in scale. It's not just about big-time success.

This realization was driven home, literally, when I invited my daughter, Megan, who was just a month or two away from college graduation, to join in on one of the discussions. "Is this discouraging to you? Is it surprising?" I asked. "Not at all. I'm in it! I just worked my butt off for four years and now they're about to throw me out of the best time of my life."

I came to see that Wes represented the canary in the coal mine—a warning to others that, not too far below the surface of success, there's a gaping hole. And I found that the bigger the goal, the bigger the hole. The biggest holes we face often have nothing to do with our jobs or our professional ambitions or plans. They have everything to do with our personal lives and the realities and challenges that we all must confront at one time or another.

Madeline Levine reminded me of this in "After the Children Have Grown," an article she wrote for the *New York Times* in 2013. Even with her background as clinician, consultant, and mother, Levine, a practicing psychologist, wasn't prepared for what would happen when she got what she wanted in terms of her children "moving into meaningful adult lives." She became "unhinged" with the graduation of her third son from college and the disruption of her "core identity" as a mother—the loss of her sense of "being needed and loved beyond reason by three breathtaking, energetic, embryonic beings."

"How odd that I should be blindsided by a sense of loss as my sons move fully into lives of their own." Some part of her, she writes, "must have known" that her sons' moves toward independence would make her "less necessary" in their lives, but "imagining our future selves tends to get neglected as we focus on our children's future."

And, I might suggest, imagining the outcome of *any* of our life's big stories tends to favor happily-ever-after endings. Like Madeline Levine, we either can't or won't envision the changes in structure, meaning, and identity that await, lurking just out of our sight. Don't dwell on the deep, dark forest, we think, and maybe it'll stay away. It seems that we all know better than to believe that things end happily ever after, but that's the story and it's sticking to us.

CHAPTER 5

A Grand Narrative of $uccess

There are stories—and then there's the big story. The Grand Narrative.

Traditionally, a Grand Narrative has been an over-arching story, a saga that inspires a people and shows them the way, both as individuals and a society. It's an explanation of experience and knowledge, a narrative that every society has, one that's relayed and retold through books and stories, tales and oral histories, songs and poetry and fables. A Grand Narrative defines a larger purpose for a group or society. It's about what might broadly be called the journey of life, and about finding truth, meaning, identity, and fulfillment along the way.

A Grand Narrative promotes and legitimizes modes of living by providing a structure for shaping life's choices. It instructs us on what is important, what to do, how to live, how to measure ourselves. Its story is always the same. It's always about the cycle of things, about the patterns and rhythms that underlie and define our lives.

A Grand Narrative both directs and reflects life, and it evolves and changes as the ethos of a culture changes. We hear this narrative, in one form or another, every day. And the way it has unfolded, what we're hearing, especially in the United States, has changed in troubling ways. Instead of striving for meaningful lives for ourselves and our children, instead of pursuing liberty and happiness, today's Grand Narrative advocates an American dream with one clear, single-minded goal: Success, with a capital S, or maybe a capital $.

Our Grand Narrative has, it seems to me, morphed into the Grand Narrative of $uccess. The "lesson" it teaches is that our lives should be dedicated to being successful, and that as long as we're pursuing success we'll have a place in the story and be valued. "Getting what we want," in this context, most often involves making money, preferably a lot of it, which then opens the doors to whatever else we might want in an endless drive to accumulate primary goods.

We see and hear this message everywhere. We're bombarded with it in the media and on the Internet, in movies and on television, in magazines and catalogues, in commercials of all sorts. We hear it in high schools and colleges and even in grade schools. Who knows, there are probably preschool administrators right now promising parents they'll get their children on the inside track to the Ivy League school of their choice—because we know where that trail leads. (In the never-too-early-to-start category, my pre-kindergarten granddaughter receives a three-page "report card"!)

I recently saw a magazine ad that presents a beautiful little girl of three or four in a fairytale setting, surrounded by butterflies and color-coordinated flowers and peeking out from behind pictures of princesses she has colored. The caption reads, in bold black letters, "I want to live." And under that, in bigger green (!) letters, "happily ever after." What do you suppose the ad was for? Crayons? No. Preschool? Not a chance. Retirement planning? That's it! Brought to you by your friendly and ubiquitous Grand Narrative of $uccess Ad Agency, where it's never too soon to get people on the bandwagon. Once you have them there, you can continue to reinforce the message, with absolutely no subtlety—like the Mercedes Benz magazine ad that reads: "Grow up. Succeed. Settle down."

We hear the message in the places where we work, or hope to: "Join us. Be successful. Get what you want." As a resident of Easy Street, you'll be able to drive the car you've always wanted, take the trip you never thought you could, and generally feel good about yourself. Finally, you'll have status and all the stuff that can go along with it. All because of success.

This Grand Narrative of Success is largely fueled by the people who make and sell the very goods and services that a striver toward success might think he or she must have—if not today, maybe next year. It's also, I think, part of our culture of stardom and celebrity, where even (or maybe especially) the suddenly successful have entourages of adorers and millions of friends who breathlessly await their next Tweet. Sudden super wealth is also attainable by winning one of the countless lotteries that millions of people pin their fading hopes on every day. How many people have thought, "If I could just win the lottery, all my problems would be solved." Such luck would be a dream come true in the land where a life's journey is not necessarily a heroic quest—but makes heroes of those who close the gap between less and more.

Luck aside, what if everything did work out according to plan and the promise of the Grand Narrative of Success? What if every project, idea, design, proposition, and wish-upon-a-star goal did exactly what it was supposed to do? What if we caught everything we chased and made out like a bandit? Ridiculous, you say? Why? Don't we believe that our plans and strategies will work? If we didn't, why would we make them in the first place? What sense would it make to invest so much of our lives and money in plans if we didn't think they were going to deliver what we want? I'm reminded of an episode of "The Twilight Zone" where a man suddenly finds himself able to see the future. He knows which horse will win the race so he bets big and wins, again and again. He plays the stock market, milks every opportunity, and acquires more and more. He can't lose. He can have everything that he thinks he wants. So, what happens? What do you think?

To greater or lesser degrees, we all buy into the idea of the Grand Narrative of Success, or at least recognize its hold on us. We experience it from the time we envy the kid next door with the cool new bike, to the time we realize that people seem more impressed by material quests than spiritual ones, to the time we understand that size does matter when it comes to homes and boats and bank accounts and portfolios.

The symbols of success are there for all to see. Not that we always admire those with the most. We might find them arrogant or elitist. We might find their words shallow or self-serving. But whatever their shortcomings, the successful people in our society are generally embraced and held up as role models and examples of what can be achieved in life— and what's possible in this land of opportunity.

That's not to say that everybody sees success in these terms—or only in these terms. A lot of people understand that success can take more than one shape. But when it comes down to making a choice between personal *spiritual* enrichment or personal *financial* enrichment, the scales are likely to tip in the direction of material gain.

CHAPTER 6

The drug of choice

The basic premise of the Grand Narrative of Success boils down to this: getting what you want makes you happy and leads to happily-ever-after.

Isn't it wonderful to have such a direct, clearly marked route to happiness? Just pop the success pill and get ready for a good and happy trip. No bad trips allowed.

Happiness is the drug of choice in the Grand Narrative of Success. The same stores that have no books on "having" offer all kinds of books with "happiness" in the title. We're addicted to pursuing happiness and all that it promises. Don't worry, be happy! Once we start getting this happiness hit, in whatever form it might take, we find that it takes more and more of it for the same buzz next time. That's what addiction does.

We keep trying to buy our way into happiness, which leads to another fundamental question: should happiness be the goal of our lives? If it's not happiness, what is it we should be after?

I find a fundamental truth in what Viktor Frankl, author of *Man's Search for Meaning*, says about happiness and the American attitude toward it. "It is characteristic of the American culture that, again and again, one is commanded and ordered to 'be happy.' But happiness cannot be pursued; it must ensue. One must have a reason to 'be happy.'" While Frankl advocates the pursuit of meaning in life, he sees American culture as more interested in the pursuit of individual happiness. And, ironically, "It is the very pursuit of happiness that thwarts happiness."

Frankl isn't saying that happiness is a distraction from a meaningful life. Rather, he cautions against pursuing mere happiness, which can't be sustained, while neglecting the pursuit of meaning, which endures and which makes human beings uniquely human.

As author George Saunders noted in his convocation speech to the 2013 graduates of Syracuse University, "'Succeeding,' whatever that might mean to you, is hard, and the need to do so constantly renews itself (success is like a mountain that keeps growing ahead of you as you hike it), and there's the very real danger that 'succeeding' will take up your whole life, while the big questions go untended. Do those things that incline you toward the big questions, and avoid the things that would reduce you and make you trivial."

Our belief system, however, our approach to life, revolves around getting what we want and thinking that doing so will make us happy—and that's all the meaning we need. How's that approach working out for people in the U.S.? According to Center for Disease Control, about 4 in 10

Americans have not found a satisfying purpose in their lives. Pursuing happiness, getting what we want, having things— all this doesn't add up to meaningful lives. Contrarily, research has shown that having purpose and meaning in life increases overall well-being and life satisfaction. It improves mental and physical health, enhances resiliency and self-esteem, and decreases the chances of depression.

Over the years, as I've met with and interviewed people who have gotten what they wanted, "happiness" has seldom been cited as the reward for their efforts. The following comments, which were made during group sessions I've led, illustrate this counterintuitive experience.

- "The more I won, the more I felt lost. More and more felt like less and less."

- "No one tells you that's what comes with victory. I think I'm developing a permanent 'who knew?' cramp in my brow."

- "I own my own company but it really owns me. My company thrives and I wither."

- "I have gotten to the point where I worry as much about success as I do failure."

- "I have so many friends out there who would be relieved, affirmed, reassured to hear what we talked about today because they are going through or have gone through the same thing."

- "That's why I wanted to be here. I need to be with people who have taken on these questions, who are living with the reality, living *with* the dream, not *for* it."

- "I actually have fantasies of leaving a note on my door: GONE HUNTING: for the real me."

- "Look at us—business people young and old, college students, housewives and others, fathers, professional people all saying essentially the same thing. We have come face to face with success and its one hell of a reward and a hell of a change and they are one and the same."

- "Before I came here I probably would have spent most of my life after success trying to figure out what's the matter with me."

- "Now we can add success to the list of things that go bump in the night."

I should add that not everybody in the groups I've met with has felt this way. Some have no interest in hearing what one called, "the Marin County blues." They have no patience for "victims" of success, as these comments illustrate.

- "You sound like a bunch of rich whiners."

- "There are people out there who would kill for what you have including this so-called problem of not knowing what you want next."

- "For you to sit here and question yourself and the tried-and-true wisdom that got you here is irresponsible."

- "Sitting in this room talking about what a challenge it is to get what you want is self-indulgent."

- "You people clearly can't handle success."

- "Success is a responsibility—live with it."

- "Life is about setting and achieving bigger and bigger goals—period."

- "You have a responsibility to your family and society to set high goals for yourself and achieve them."

- "Life is simple. You set a goal, it gives you purpose, and you know who you are."

Take a closer look at that last statement: "*Life is simple. You set a goal, it gives you purpose, and you know who you are.*" Have you found this to be true in your own life? Have the goals you've set given you purpose and identity? Is life really this "simple"? The statement was made by someone who apparently thinks so.

And what makes it so simple, to him and so many others? The Grand Narrative of Success, which provides an uncomplicated formula for making it through life: if you dedicate yourself to being successful by constantly pursuing success, you'll have a place in society and be valued as a person. If you don't dedicate yourself to this, well, things won't be quite as simple. You'll be on your own.

The Grand Narrative of Success promises three things that all of us seek in our lives.

Structure. Living according to the Grand Narrative's precepts gives our lives a shape, a framework from which to proceed. It leads to networks of relationships, a structure of rhythms and routines, a membership in a collective for pursuing shared goals. It's a design for our days and our dreams.

Meaning. Adhering to the goals of the Grand Narrative of Success, being part of it, attaches a meaning to our lives. When the question "What should I be doing with my life?" is posed, the answer is right there in front of us: constantly striving for (*pick any or all*) achievement, acquisition, and acclaim.

Identity. By giving us structure and meaning, the Grand Narrative of Success provides us with an identity; as noted above, "you know who you are." When someone asks who you are and what you do, your answer is right there: "I'm a (*pick a profession or occupation*). I'm really interested in (*pick a next goal or ambition*). How about you?" It's how we are known to ourselves and others. I Think-Pad, therefore, I am. If nobody calls are you there?

Ultimately, the Grand Narrative of Success promises freedom to do what you want. For many of the people I've met, that freedom means playing lots of golf, traveling to faraway places, eating well, and dealing with the challenges of leisure time. We in the U.S. like to brag about our freedom. We sing its praises. We let it ring!

CHAPTER 7

Suffer the children?

There's another aspect of the Grand Narrative of Success that should raise eyebrows: its impact on our children. Maybe you're a parent putting huge pressure on your kids to "succeed." Or maybe you're a son or daughter feeling, and trying to deal with, that pressure. Here are a few statements that illustrate the kinds of things I hear all the time.

- "I think we've been led to believe the story because they need to scare you. They think it gives you incentives. They teach us that since we were kids."

- "It's been drilled in my head since the beginning: Have a goal, achieve the goal."

- "It's what we're counting on if we study hard, get good grades, ace the SATs, get a good job, climb the ladder. If you don't, it's your own fault."

- "I don't know about the rest of you, but I know a lot of people whose lives were ruined and who were miserable trying to outdo their parents."

- "God, I'd hate to be my kid."

America is a rags-to-riches culture, founded by people who came here to make a better life for themselves and their children. That dogged determination is a part of American life and lore. Each generation works hard and sacrifices so their children can lead a better life than they did. The socio-economic distance between parents and children has been the metric that matters. Kids can't just be their parents; they must outdo them. And if they don't climb the ladder, it's their own fault.

As a parent, I've been guilty of perpetrating this kind of pressure. When my daughter, as a high school student, voiced her skepticism about joining the world of getting ahead, about doing what others expect of her and wondering why she had to, I remember giving her an answer straight out of the book of the Grand Narrative of Success, something like, "You'll do it because if you don't you'll find yourself on the outside looking in. If you don't follow this tried-and-true course, you'll go off the rails." I can still see the look she gave me, the kind of give-me-a-break grimace that can drive a parent to distraction. In such a case as this, it should also drive a parent to take a fresh look at the whole proposition, as, ultimately, it did with me.

If it takes enormous courage for adults to ignore the expectations and evaluations of others, how tough is it for our kids? What's happening to those whose parents have achieved the affluence that so many of us seek and admire?

One study, published in 2012 in the *Journal of Research on Adolescence*, shows that, in some unexpected ways, what's happening is not what the Grand Narrative of Success says should happen. The study looks at two groups of adolescents: those living in affluent neighborhoods and those living in middle-class neighborhoods. It found that boys from the affluent areas had higher rates of delinquency than those from the middle-class areas. Girls in affluent surroundings were found to have higher levels of anxiety and depression than those in middle-class settings.

Might these unhappy youths be examples of the "rich whiners" mentioned earlier? Or might they be a signal that the journey to success is fraught with troubles we're not told about? Here's a quick test: if your kids, no matter what age, could understand the information and ideas offered in this book would you want them to read it? Why? Why not? It's a question I've asked hundreds of CEOs—never fails to start a lively conversation.

CHAPTER 8

"What are you going to do?"

There are two questions that we've all been asked. One is, "What do you do?" The other, when the answer to the first question isn't sufficiently specific, is, "What are you going to do?" We also ask others—and, less openly, ourselves—these same questions. Where would cocktail parties be without such words to fall back on? "Hi, Rick. And what do you do?" "I'm a psychologist and I'm currently working on a book about what happens when people get what they want. And you?" We're all supposed to have a ready answer to such questions. If we don't, the conversation might quickly turn awkward, with a touch of pity thrown in. "Well, good luck finding something. I mean, well, yes, best of luck. Take care."

While perhaps well intentioned, "What are you going to do?" may be the last question a person wants to hear, and hear, and hear, and answer, and answer, and answer. Here's what someone I've met with had to say about it. "I got back home from a two-year hitch in the Peace Corps and everywhere I went there was that question: 'What are you going to do? Great to have you back, what are you doing to do?' I didn't even get home before that question hit me. I had two flights and the conversation with the person next to me basically went like this: 'Where are you headed?' 'Home from the Peace Corps.' 'What are you going to do?'"

The same kind of "conversation" happens in all kinds of circumstances when a person has gotten what he or she wanted. I've heard about a lot of them: Congratulations on the new baby! What are you going to do? You're taking a sabbatical? What are you going to do? You sold your company, quit your job, graduated from school, survived cancer, inherited some money, got divorced, got married, dropped your kid off at college. What are you going to do?

We're so used to having something to do that as soon as we aren't doing something tangible and, preferably, profitable, we can feel like outcasts from the Grand Narrative of Success. We might even feel like (to use the popular phrase) "losers." What have we lost? Oh, nothing much, really—just our identity and meaning, just a structure for our lives. One of my clients, who had sold his company, got so tired of being asked what he was going to do that he decided to create a "cover," something to tell everyone, and himself, about what he was doing (while he was actually trying to figure out what he really wanted to do).

Such feelings of loss have a way of showing up when we least expect them—often as an aftermath of a great win, a profitable sale, a major hike completed. I expect loss to be quietly poised to ambush me once I get what I want by finishing this book. And I'll still be surprised by the power of its effect on me. Go figure.

Let's face it. Being an active participant in the Grand Narrative of Success quells all the questions about what you're going to do next. You know what you'll do: You'll jump back into the arena of expected achievement, moving quickly and surely to the next big goal. You'll rejoin a familiar race. You'll have ready answers for everybody, including yourself, about what you're going to do, and how you're going to do it. You'll get more of what you want and be happy as a result.

All courtesy of the Grand Narrative of Success.

CHAPTER 9

The chance to make a choice

The Grand Narrative of Success is a kind of game where no one cares about your last at-bat. (Please excuse this and any other sports metaphors that I might attempt.) It's all about what you're going to do the next time you're up. Predictably, getting what you want temporarily ends your place in the story of the Grand Narrative. When you get what you want, you're done, and you have nowhere to go but to a place where you're positioned to get more of what you want. That gets you back into the game. It gives you another at-bat.

When we don't find that new place, we may feel like we've run out of the story, but in fact the story has run out on us. Our current Grand Narrative is too limited because it only takes us to "more." It's too small because it has nothing to offer us after we reach our goal but to repeat ourselves. So we use proven processes to accomplish familiar goals that give us more. The problem? The more we *get* what we want, the harder it is to *know* what we want. And when we don't know what we want, we fall back into wanting more. Feeding the appetite of the Grand Narrative of $uccess creates hunger.

What's a person to do?

If we opt out of the Grand Narrative of Success, we're out of easy answers to the question of what we should be doing with our lives. Instead, we'll find ourselves some- where in Stephen Sondheim's woods, after happily-ever- after, in an uncharted place, but also a place of possibilities.

Maybe "opt out" overstates what it takes to get a grip on our headlong pursuit of success/happiness. Opt out implies a total rejection of the idea of success and what it can bring. It can sound like living off the grid is the only viable alterna- tive. Not so. In fact, it's my belief that success, if we allow it to, can lead us to explore life's timeless questions. More about that later.

Instead of "opt out," how about "seriously question"? Or "critically evaluate"? The point being that instead of blindly following the Grand Narrative, we should at least view it with enough skepticism to realize that there might be better ways to find what we're looking for.

Maybe you're wondering, how did we get from hiking the Camino de Santiago to maneuvering through the Grand Narrative? What's the connection between one guy complet- ing a cross-country trek and another contemplating what to do now that he's sold his business and has plenty of money?

One connection is that they've both been disconnected— from life as they've known it and the structure, meaning, and identity that came with it. Eventually they will both recon- nect with their lives in new ways, and as they do, they'll both have the opportunity to make choices about what that means.

At the end of their journeys, each venturer is confronted with the choice of where to go from there, what to do now that an end has come and left open a door to something else. As I've noted, while much of the work I've done has involved people who are well positioned financially, I've also dealt with plenty of people who don't have such a safety net, and that's not their worry anyway. They're working through the aftereffects of all kinds of changes and challenges that have resulted from getting what they want, or thought they wanted.

My focus isn't just on rich guys retiring and having leisure time to consider their options. It's also on anyone who completes a major or important effort (a degree, a stint in the service, an attempt at marriage, a book, the Camino) and, when it's over, when they're free from it, even though they might not want to be, are presented with the opportunity to take a fresh look at things, including the direction of their lives.

It's a time to ask, in Carl Sandburg's words, "Where to? What next?"

CHAPTER 10

The hero's journey, and ours

There's another journey, beyond the call to success that I think sheds a clarifying light on the nature of the trip we're all on. Part of a story that pervades cultural narratives everywhere, it helps us better understand and appreciate where our own journeys are taking us.

The story of this—the hero's journey—was brought to the world's attention in the middle of the 20th century by Joseph Campbell in his book *The Hero with a Thousand Faces,* a work that has affected the way that many of us, including me, think about the stories of our own lives.

In it, Campbell, citing mythologies from cultures worldwide, shows how people everywhere have virtually the same heroic journey tucked away in their subconscious. He says that there is basically only one story: the grand story of our lives. It's told in many different ways, but ultimately every story is either a retelling of this story or of certain aspects of it. (Or, as my friend Linda, who walked the Camino with her

82-year-old father, put it, "Each peregrino is every peregrino.")

For all the differences that might seem to divide people, Campbell finds that striking similarities unite these stories. Stories with roots thousands of years old share a common fundamental structure and message. The hero's journey, in one form or another, is in every great story, its pattern underlying all human experiences.

As Campbell states, "A hero ventures forth from the world of common day into a region of supernatural wonder. Fabulous forces are there encountered and a decisive victory is won. The hero comes back from this mysterious adventure with the power to bestow boons on his fellow man."

The hero's journey is composed of cycles of separation, initiation, and return that occur over the course of our lives. It is marked by clear stages, including an initial call, the crossing of a threshold, a temptation, a boon acquired by the hero, and various elements of a return and final triumph. The hero faces trials and risks and, in meeting and surviving them, undergoes a kind of rebirth or awakening and discovers, in a sense, himself. Armed with this self-knowledge, he returns with the power to make the world a better place.

The path the hero takes reflects the formula for rites of passage—separation, initiation, return (Campbell also calls this pattern departure, fulfillment, return)—that is found in cultures worldwide. In a sense, we—not just "heroes" but all of us—must "venture forth" and face the unknown with courage and strength. Returning home means returning to ourselves—a symbolic return to being a more complete human being. If we understand the journey pattern, we'll be better able to face difficulties and use our life experiences to become the people we want to be. Instead of "want to be" we psychologists might say "were meant to be" as a result of our lifelong journey of individuation. The process of development suggests an unfolding to reveal what is hidden within. While the Grand Narrative of $uccess uses imagery and language of planning and building, the timeless way is discovery.

The hero's journey demands that we face ourselves and our fears—and that we discover our own meaning, our authentic identity, away from the comforts of home and family and the known world. To find ourselves, we have to, in a sense, lose ourselves. This is, indeed, a heroic quest. This call to action has noble intentions, and it has been embedded in us for centuries and centuries. Venturing forth and returning victorious is, as people like to say these days, "part of our DNA."

Campbell reminds us that we will have tests, trials, and "dragons" (our inner fears working against us) to face on our quest. He notes that while "we all operate in our society in relation to a system," the big question is whether or not the system is "going to eat you up and relieve you of your humanity. Living in terms of a system is a threat to our lives." My favorite reminder of how our creations become our masters comes from the artist Robert Irwin: "People working through structures become structures working through people." How do we go from expressing identity and meaning in structures to deriving meaning and identity from those creations? Why do some people come to do the Camino while others come to let the Camino do them?

In his oft-quoted phrase, Campbell's advice is to "follow your bliss."

"Follow your bliss and the universe will open doors for you where there were only walls," he says. "If the work that you're doing is the work that you chose to do because you enjoy it, then that's bliss, but if you think, 'oh, I couldn't be that' that's your dragon."

The hero's journey is not about those with the most primary goods. "The statement of need and want must come from you," Campbell says. "Don't align yourself with a programmatic life. The world is full of people who have stopped listening to themselves."

Life is one long journey to discover who we really are, why we are here, and what we are meant to do. This process of self-discovery can be confusing and painful, but it's essential in developing a deeper sense of ourselves. Every situation that confronts us with something new or that forces us to reevaluate our thinking, behavior, or perspective presents us with possibilities for insight and growth.

The hero's journey represents such a high-minded possibility, an antidote to the stuff and status that the Grand Narrative of Success promotes.

CHAPTER 11

Is that all there is?

When was the last time you felt you were in a position to take a fresh look at the direction of your life—and to do something about it? Was it soon after you had gotten something that you had wanted, something that you had worked for (or maybe lucked into)? Had you assumed that getting it would bring about the opportunity for a new and improved version of yourself? Last question: Did you take a step on such a new path or did you remain on familiar, established terrain?

OK, so I lied. One more question: Did you ever ask yourself, "Is that all there is"?

Believers in the Grand Narrative of Success, those who find that its promises hold up over time, would answer, "Yes, that's all that there is. What more *should* there be?" Here's how a participant in one of my discussion groups put it: "*Get a goal, get a purpose, get a vision, and get going back into all those great things you worked so hard to have. It's all laid out for you. It may be a formula, as someone called it, but it works. Look around. Where would you be, where would we all be if it didn't work, or if every time you were successful you just chucked everything and said, 'I'm just going to go off and do what I want even if right now I have no idea what that is.'"* In other words, you either choose to live according to the tenets of the Grand Narrative of Success or you don't, in which case you're out there without a guide. And who wants that?

I've found that a lot of people do, although it may have taken them a while to recognize it. They want to be out there, even though it may be scary and humbling, because they're looking for something more than they've been able to find by following the usual recipes for success and the happiness it promises. They are among those who ask, "Is that all there is"? And aren't willing to accept "yes" for an answer. At times people will say to me, "I climbed to the top of the ladder and then realized it was leaning up against the wrong wall." My question to them is: "Is it a wrong wall problem, or a top rung problem?"

There's something else that I've heard from a lot of people: the word "freedom." Often, it's about their desire to be free *from* certain things—a job, a relationship, a promise. "If I could just be free from what's weighing on me, then I'd be able to (*fill in the blank*)"—one of those if/then scenarios I talked about earlier. Less often, I hear people talk about the freedom *to*, as in the freedom to live life on their own terms. It's seems easier for people to enumerate the things they'd like to be free from than to specify what they'd like to be free to.

That's at least partly due to their not knowing what they'd do with such freedom. How would they handle it? Might it lead them directly into Sondheim's woods, where the trail is unmarked and the outcome unknown? In a word, yes. It could, and that's exactly what appeals to those who ask, "Is that all there is"? And are ready to face the task of finding out if, indeed, that *is* all there is. That same lack of a clear direction is what immobilizes those whose fear or distrust of the woods keeps them within the safety of the known.

Having the freedom to choose is both a reward and a challenge, a gift and a burden. Choosing is self-defining. We say we want it, but do we really? Are we ready for it? Are we ready to embrace the freedom *to* live life on our own terms? Or are we more at ease with the freedom *from* the unknown that the well-traveled path seems to offer?

Are we ready—will we ever be ready—to take the first step on a hero's journey?

CHAPTER 12

Making choices,
Searching for meaning

Some people have the freedom to choose on a grand scale. People like Wes enjoy the luxury of not having to scramble for money as they look to new possibilities. (Wes, however, found little solace in this after he got what he wanted.) From our viewpoint, they are above the fray, well positioned to make the big choices, such as whether to rejoin the Grand Narrative of Success or to look in other directions—to be able to choose without negative consequences.

Most folks, though, and maybe you're one of them, don't have such an advantage. They're spending all their energy keeping up with the demands, financial and otherwise, of the known world. They have neither the time nor the where-withal to be gazing into a future that seems beyond reach. Their freedom to choose seems limited to more mundane matters—to everyday life, not out-there aspirations.

And yet I've found that whether they're living large or small, thoughtful people have a common desire to be true to themselves as they pursue their goals. They want the opportunity to make free and enlightened choices about what comes next. Whether it's a baby boomer who's looking for an alternative to what's he's been doing for 30 or 40 years, or a millennial who can't see herself sitting in a cubicle, the people I've met with and interviewed have a real need to find something that feels in sync with their beliefs, skills, and passions.

Ultimately, their search is for meaning. Sometimes it's a case of better late than never. Always it's a question of how. And answering that question—solving the how-to-go-forward quandary—depends to a great degree on one key choice: do we continue to follow the prescribed path of the Grand Narrative of Success or do we create our own path, our own narrative? We can lead our lives in accordance with either one. Neither is a guarantee of anything, including success or happiness or meaning.

Choice #1

Get into (or get back into) the Grand Narrative of Success. You'll probably get plenty of support for making this your choice. It's the seemingly safe one, but beware of bad advice, simple answers, and what has been called the "tyranny of the should": you should be happy, always, forever; you should always have a goal, a focus, a bigger mountain to climb, a vision. You should always go forward at full throttle. This choice begins with setting a goal and following a known structure to pursue and achieve success. This gives meaning to one's life and creates an identity based on the success of the pursuit.

Choice #2

Create your own story; be the author of your own narrative. Make this your choice and get ready for some naysayers. These could include parents and children, lawyers and accountants, poker-playing buddies and portfolio-carrying business colleagues. They all might claim to be worried about you. This choice begins with establishing who you are (identity) and what you care about (meaning). From this, you determine the structures that will allow you to live in accordance with the identity and meaning that you are establishing for yourself.

There's nothing inherently better about either of these choices. It's a matter of personal choice—a decision based on, among other things, one's ambitions, motivations, and satisfaction (or lack of) with the current state of things, with the rightness of the current path. Either choice provides the opportunity to take a thoughtful look ahead and to take the first step toward what awaits.

When I brought up this idea of choosing one or the other in one of my group discussions, one man, looking puzzled and a bit irritated, called out, "You mean I have to choose between the Grand Narrative of Success and my own story?" It was a good and fair question. I could sense his skepticism about having to make such an either/or decision.

So I said something like this: "What matters is how we engage with our choice, what we do with it. One person's decision to stay with what choice #1 offers can make just as much sense as another's decision to slip behind the curtain that hides choice #2. And it's not as if making this choice is all-pervasive—that it means either living on or off the grid of the Grand Narrative at all times and in all circumstances. You can begin to author your own narrative even as you continue to seek "success" via known routes. In fact, success can put you in a great position to explore the bigger questions of life. Opportunities for self-awareness and self-development don't travel on just one path."

"So, Rick," you might ask, "is that why you keep referring to your hike on that trail over in Spain—because it's an example of a self-building journey of discovery? If you are, how about telling us more?"

Coincidentally, I was just about to.

CHAPTER 13

Inklings of a new reality

I'd like to begin prior to my year-long obsessive-compulsive preparation for the journey—back to the time when the idea to hike the Camino was first, as they say, "entering my consciousness." Because that was what it was like. I didn't invite it in. I wasn't looking for an adventure, at least not one like this. I was 70 years old, 25 pounds overweight, and tangled up in the responsibilities of my personal and professional life. I didn't have the time or inclination to become a "peregrino."

And then, a slowly bubbling idea began to surface. Where it came from, I'm not sure. Maybe beneath my outwardly contented self was another guy I hadn't been listening to. I mean, who wants to hear, "You're getting old, Rick. The clock ticks ever faster, but you move ever slower." Or maybe it arose from my interest in maps. Since I was a kid I've enjoyed looking at them; I like the idea of being able to look down on the earth from above. John Steinbeck loved maps. In *Travels with Charley*, he spends hours with them, usually after dinner, mapping out his next move on his cross-country heroic journey to rediscover America. Maps hold a kind of promise, a reminder of all that there is. They're a call to go somewhere, to do something.

When I got my "call" to hike the Camino, the slowly bubbling idea finally surfaced. It didn't bring me to my knees in awe. A bright light didn't blaze by. It was more like a calm voice in my ear, "You're going to do this. This is the right thing to do." Feeling a surge of energy and expectation, I was sure that this voice was right. If people have epiphanies, then this would probably qualify.

When I meet with people who have gotten what they want I like to bring up this idea of listening to what's within us. I call these inner voices "inklings." You might choose another word—intuition, instinct, gut feeling. But in the context of my work—where people are often struggling with what to do next—I talk about inklings as in "inklings of a new reality."

The people I work with are looking for something beyond what they have, to new possibilities. I encourage them to carefully consider any inklings they might have. An inkling doesn't always come in an instant. People can have longstanding inklings, feelings in their bones that occasionally surface and are, for whatever reason, dismissed.

Inklings, which are nonlinear and nonformulaic, can compel us to action. They need to be heard. But while they stir up vitality and excitement, they can also incite fear, a hesitancy to act that's brought on by a lack of confidence or a tendency toward worst-case-scenario thinking. I have watched people run roughshod over their inklings to get to an easier answer to the "now what?" question. We reject our honest answers, stomp on our heart's desires, and then wonder why we can't find our passion.

I think that such fear is an expression of an undeveloped part of ourselves that needs to be tended to. It's what happens when "realism" turns out to be a way of avoiding, rather than facing, things.

Inklings can lead to the first step of a journey to that undeveloped part of us. They can help us begin consulting maps that chart the territory beyond success, maps that we ourselves must draw.

CHAPTER 14

On my blindness

I know I'm different since walking the Camino, even if I can't tell you exactly how. I do know this (and so does my wife): the me that started isn't the me who is writing this book. Before I went, my tendency was to be in a fast-forward mode, always. Like Satchel Paige, I didn't look back for fear that something might be gaining on me. With my eyes on the future—on what's next—I often wasn't very good at seeing, really seeing, what was right in front of me.

I remember walking across barren ground that went on for miles along the Camino. It's part of the Meseta region and it takes a week to traverse. Crunching under my boots was a monochromatic moonscape, a place that seemed devoid of anything but rocks and gravel. No trees or bushes or blades of grass mitigated the starkness of the scene. With every step, my impatience with this part of the journey grew. I became the kind of grumpy hiker that nobody wants to be around. Finally, my friend Mike, the poor guy who was walking with me, grew tired of my pissing-and-moaning exasperation and occasional declaration that I didn't know I had signed up for a moon walk.

"Can't you see what's here?" he asked. "You've walked all this way and not noticed these?" He knelt down and touched one of the tiny, delicate, fuchsia-colored blossoms growing from nothingness, little beauties that I'd been breezing by. I had been so concerned with what wasn't there that I was completely oblivious to what was.

Such blindness is an example of a scarcity mentality, an affliction brought on by being so preoccupied with what isn't that we can't see what is. It's an inability—as we pursue distant goals—to be present in the now. In the process, we lose our appreciation of life's everyday wonders, and maybe even our own dreams. It's a price that's often paid as we strive to get what we want. On the Camino that day, this realization startled me. It also humbled me, which is not easy to do.

Later, as I thought about the larger implications, it occurred to me that such a scarcity mentality is a basic tenet of the Grand Narrative of Success, which tells us that we can never have enough and that what we have now is merely a step toward getting more. This mentality isn't just a focus on what we don't have. It's also a worry and fear that what we do have, we could lose. That fear keeps people on the Grand Narrative train of success. It stops them from considering an alternative way to travel.

Often I ask clients and members of groups that I speak to this question: How will you know when you have enough? (And, *you*, how will you know when you have enough?) Here's my answer to my own question: You have enough when you say you do. Until you can say you do, you will never have enough.

CHAPTER 15

The question that isn't asked

More than any particular event along the Camino, the entire experience—from first inkling to final step—showed me the larger truth: the huge difference between the fantasy of what we seek and the reality of what we get. Fantasy is simple, a focusing illusion. Reality is complex, an ongoing pattern of loss and gain.

Focused on and driven by their own illusions, travelers on the Camino typically ask each other one or all of four questions:

- Where did you start?

- Where are you going?

- How's it going?

- Why did you come?

Whatever trail you're on, these are worthy questions. But what could be a fifth question—*What do you think will happen once you get to Santiago?*—never gets asked, at least not in my experience. I know that I never asked anyone that question, not even myself. That's one reason I was so taken aback when I did get to Santiago. It was only after the fact, after I had gotten what I wanted, that the question was answered for me, as I told you in the preface, and it wasn't what I had expected. My illusion was shattered by the reality of what I had lost by getting what I wanted. It wasn't the first time this has happened and it won't be the last.

Let me relate one of those other experiences. I can still clearly remember walking out of the room where I had finished the final defense of my doctoral dissertation. It was the last hurdle in a long and often seemingly endless obstacle course on the way to being welcomed into the "community of scholars." The final handshake, "Congratulations, Doctor Eigenbrod," and there I was walking down familiar hallways looking and feeling like a fighter who had just barely beaten the count. So long in coming, so much work and anxiety. I had walked in as a graduate student and left as a Ph.D. I had made it and, by doing so, had lost it. Now what?

I was a mess for quite a while. It's hard to handle being a mess when everyone around you is celebrating your success, expecting you to be happy, and asking, "What are you going to do now?" It's even harder when that initial letdown continues long after the party is over.

But try telling this "problem" to somebody. If your dissertation defense had failed and you were a mess, you could find plenty of people who would understand and empathize. But if you tell them that your defense was flawless and you've been a mess ever since, forget about understanding or sympathy. Except, as in my case, if you're lucky enough to have someone (for me, my wife) who's more tolerant and less judgmental. But even she, for a while, would have a hard time dealing with me. And would again, with each "I did it!" that I shouted after the Camino trip was over.

Time helps. Time and confronting the questions of "Where to? What next?

CHAPTER 16

Becoming your own narrator

S o, due to some combination of work, study, stubbornness, initiative, and luck, you get what you want. Something big in terms of what's important to you. You've been seeking what you now have because you saw some advantage in having it. Maybe it puts you in a place where you'll have more opportunity to do what you want to. Change jobs. Write a book. Get married. Start a business.

I think there's a greater opportunity beyond this: the chance to begin to create your own story, to be the author of your own narrative. I brought this idea up several pages back as an alternative to another story: the Grand Narrative of Success, authored by no one but endorsed by all those who would have you follow it. Not that there's anything wrong with that!

In fact, the Grand Narrative relieves us of a huge responsibility: answering the hard questions. Uncertain? Confused? Conflicted? Not even sure of what the questions are? No problem. The Grand Narrative of Success has the answers you need. Be productive, benefit the group, get the goodies. You *have* to be productive. The narrative is cruel to the non-productive members of society, dismissive of those who can't or won't devote themselves to following its principles. More and more corporations are calculating the productivity of individual employees, in both factories and offices, making it a key measure of worth. We have metrics to measure productivity on national, regional, and local levels. We're even finding ways to measure it in our schools.

I'm not diminishing the value of productivity or the necessity of seeking to improve it. I'm just cautioning against assuming that the mentality that measures economic and social success should be the same mentality by which we measure our *lives*. Whatever brief time you allow yourself outside this narrative of endless striving (maybe soon after you've gotten what you want), you can use to explore and choose other ways to measure the *value* of your life.

Such introspection is one way that people can begin to author their own narratives, to make graceful and thoughtful transitions to what's next. As we move through life, reshaping and refining who we are and what we care about, being our own narrators allows us to choose in terms that are in sync with our goals, passions, and beliefs. It means pursuing our goals and developing our identities on our own terms and according to our own metrics.

You don't need to *set* goals; you can *discover* them by authoring your own narrative. As a self-author, you travel like a discoverer, not a navigator. Navigators know where they're going and how to get there using other people's maps. Discoverers set their own course and draw their own maps. They let the landscape tell them where to go. Along the way, even when they don't know exactly where they're going, they find themselves seeing more than if they had chosen a predetermined destination.

Self-authors define "success" in their own terms. They expand the common definition (e.g., wealth, prosperity, stature) to include personal outcomes (e.g., wisdom, empathy, contentment, long-lived purpose) that can't be formulated by committee or measured by productivity or demographic studies. Defining success is an act of *self*-definition. We reveal what matters to us by the way we choose to define ourselves.

I've heard lots of people talk, with regret, about how much has *happened* to them over the years and how little they have *made* things happen. I think that authoring one's own story can help prevent this feeling that someone or something else is pulling the strings in our lives. When we're our own authors, we write before and live into it.

You can become your own author if you want to, and you don't have to know where you're going before you get started. You just have to know that you're ready to listen to yourself. This recognition might begin as an inkling—of a newly discovered reality, a new sense of self.

CHAPTER 17

Making our own choices

E ven though the choices we have made eventually make us, they don't make us in stone. We need to realize this. We also need to realize that unless we find a new framework for choosing, we will take what's easy and familiar because it's easy and familiar. We need to see our choices as expressions of our lives at the moment. Life requires of us a constant process of making choices that are current, free, and enlightened. We are all works in progress.

Ultimately, our choices determine how satisfied we are with the way we're living our lives. But choices, important ones, are not easy to confront (even though having them is far preferable to not having them). As we get older, and maybe wiser, recapturing our sense of choice can be even tougher. The fundamental challenge is to become more conscious of the choices we make (or have made) and to be aware that they are reflections of the way we define and refine ourselves.

We assume that success will change our circumstances but not ourselves. So we try to put our life back together much the way it was and so miss a tremendous opportunity to not only redesign our life structures, the externals, but also to change our sense of who we are, which is the essence of individual development. We need to separate ourselves from what we do to know who we are.

Success offers us what was always ours: the right and privilege to reexamine and reevaluate what's important. Each success can be part of a series of opportunities to understand ourselves and inform our choices going forward. After success, we are free to do what we were always free to do: define ourselves as we are now. The task is to get current with ourselves, or as someone put it, "to own up to what's me and carve away what's not me."

Success is not where the hero's journey ends; it's where it begins. This process requires an inward journey, one that presents us with the chance to ask some big questions:

- Who am I now? (Identity)

- What do I care about now? (Meaning)

- How will I express it? (Structure)

Remember George Saunders' advice to the 2013 graduates of Syracuse University: "There's the very real danger that 'succeeding' will take up your whole life, while the big questions go untended. Do those things that incline you toward the big questions, and avoid the things that would reduce you and make you trivial."

Never underestimate the power of the big question. It's the question that moves us forward. And, again, the first question isn't "Who am I?" It's "Who am I now?" It's one of those big questions you get to face when you get what you want. And, as John O'Donohue wrote, "The question holds the lantern."

Here's another big one: "What's the measure of a life? More importantly, what's the measure of mine?" I've heard it said that we measure what we can, not what's important. How will you measure your life? By what metric?

Identity building and refinement is a lifelong trek that's catalyzed in many ways, particularly by the critical event of success. Understanding who we are and what we want requires a clear view of ourselves, our motives, and the identity we seek. Some people might call this journey selfish or narcissistic. I think that when it's undertaken with honesty, conviction, and good intention it is noble and even heroic, a boon to both ourselves and others.

CHAPTER 18

Living freely in spaciousness

In my experience, the people who succeed in creating their own narrative, those who use it to explore and direct their lives, share a common trait: the faith and courage to stand within emptiness for a while.

What kind of emptiness? The kind that's the natural result of getting what we want. It's the void—the temporary loss of structure, meaning, and identity—that follows the fullness of accomplishment and achievement. That's how it feels to a lot of people: like floating in a void, like being lost without a map.

Some people never find their way out of the void, but maybe that's okay with them. Maybe just groovin' in the void has been their lifelong dream. Or, more likely, they figure out that the best way to deal with it is to choose to fill it up again with more of the same stuff they always have.

Others don't try to fill it up again. They see, or learn, that this void is not nothing. It is something, ironically, that we say we want and work so hard to achieve: freedom and spaciousness. But, like Sondheim's woods, such freedom and spaciousness can be tough to deal with. It can scare us away, make us quickly retreat to the fortress of the familiar. As poet and author David Whyte writes, "Human beings seem to have the amazing ability to turn any sudden gift of freedom and spaciousness into its exact opposite. The mantle of possibility descends upon us and, instead of warming and emboldening, covers our face and our eyes." To resist the temptation to allow our face and eyes to be covered requires faith in ourselves and the courage to stand within emptiness, to see that emptiness is an opportunity, not a void.

Choosing to author our own stories gives us a focus for working with the freedom and spaciousness we find when we get what we want. It helps us create a framework that's grounded in self-building, not success-building. Learning to make the most of living within freedom and spaciousness will likely require some changes in the way we typically look at and deal with things.

"Spaciousness! What's that?" That outburst got a reaction from the other CEOs in the room that showed they wondered what the hell it was, too.

I was trying to offer perspective on the emptiness that comes with the fullness when we get what we want. It's what the phrase "the bigger the goal, the bigger the hole" refers to. While I like it because it rhymes, I like it more because it's true. The word hole itself connotes emptiness, darkness, loss. It's a void, a vacuum, an absence. In fact, that's how we experience it. The disruption to the status quo when we get what we want comes to some extent from what's *not* there anymore. The goal, the drive, the routines, the "friends" gone. So that's how people feel it, see it, and talk about it.

In my presentation I was trying to pull off some "cognitive reframing"—messing with their heads and changing their minds, essentially what I've been trying to do throughout this book. Offer them what this book offers you. But they were having none of it. I was trying to blow their minds and they simply blew me off. I'm kind of used to it by now.

In meetings where I speak to people who aren't CEOs, I hear similar guffaws. "I just get upset listening to you because the rich guys can afford spaciousness. I got a new wife and baby, and I don't have time for this California crap!" One guy even pulled out his electronic calendar to prove that he has no time for anything more in his life. "See? It's filled!"

"Spaciousness! What's that?" That question got me thinking more deeply about the whole idea. For one thing, I realize, people equate *spaciousness* with *space*. It's a point of confusion I run into a lot. Space can be filled. (Space is limited, so be sure to hurry!) Spaciousness can't be filled. (Spaciousness is unlimited, so take your time!) Spaciousness is a region of possibility. It offers us a new vista, the chance for a more expansive view of ourselves, what we care about, and how we might express it.

Spaciousness is *not*:

- a blank spot on your calendar

- nothing going on

- what's around you

- the absence of something

- a void

Spaciousness *is*:

- an open calendar

- being receptive to all that's going on

- what's in you

- something

- a way to be

Spaciousness can be cultivated. It grows best without competition so start by eliminating what hinders it. Here are some suggestions, some reminders of what we've already talked about.

Let go of linearity. Life is not linear, no matter how much we try to convince ourselves that it is. Life is not the shortest distance between two points. When we try to live our lives as though we can set a point out in time and go directly there, we set ourselves up to be blindsided at every turn. There's no straight line between success and anything, including peace of mind, contentment, fulfillment, and self-development.

Let go of the need to be in control. We have control mechanisms, control systems, and control freaks. Our need to control comes from what we're trying to prevent. When we try to stop all deviations in order to get a straight line, we lose out on all the other possibilities of getting there. It's the meanderings that make the trip interesting.

Let go of scarcity. Don't let yourself fall victim to the voices that say you don't have enough, you'll never have enough. Don't let those same voices convince you to stay put by issuing dire warnings about losing what you do have if you try something else. Don't find yourself rushing ahead focused on getting what you don't have. Don't pass by the beautiful little flowers along the path.

Let go of goal setting. Everyone knows you need a goal. Right? Wrong! We made it up. Or rather, the Grand Narrative of Success made it up, and we act as if it's true. Western civilization won't collapse because you don't have a goal. You don't need to *set* goals. You can *discover* them by moving along your own path of energy, interest, and curiosity to wherever it takes you.

Live with the questions. We think of questions as problems and answers as solutions. We want to throttle questions into submission. We forget that they foster exploration and learning even when they're not answered. Suggestion: live with the questions. Success allows you to trade in your old questions for better ones.

What's next?

When I ask people how they want to live their lives, especially after they've gotten what they wanted, I hear all kinds of interesting answers: "To live my life so that I am interesting to myself." "To not walk through the doors that others open for me." "To go where I'm really needed." "To live nobly."

I never hear anything like, "To die with the most toys," even though "He who dies with the most toys *wins*" was a popular Silicon Valley mantra that defined success in the 1980s and 90s, when it appeared on bumper stickers and t-shirts (and not just in California). Before long, another tagline began showing up: "He who dies with the most toys *still dies.*"

Well, there's no getting around that. We can't take our toys with us. Still, the temptation, the pressure, is toward accumulating them as a measure of our success, as visible evidence of a life well lived (and properly financed). The tempter, of course, is the Grand Narrative of Success, telling us over and over to stay the course, stick with the familiar, avoid wandering off the straight line.

It takes courage not to follow these directives. It takes curiosity and a strong sense of self to look within for answers to the questions that the Grand Narrative isn't concerned with and would rather we not ask. (Who am I now? What do I care about now? How will my life express this now?)

When we author our own stories, we can ask ourselves anything. We can explore our lives with unfettered honesty, free of dogma and preconceived answers. But even though we might intuitively recognize this opportunity, even though we might have an inkling of the possibilities it presents, we're nevertheless constrained by the "reality" of what is. We have a hard time thinking that a new reality can be discovered within us.

I've written this book to open people's eyes to the possibility of making that discovery. I don't have any magic formulas to follow. I'm just saying that we are always free to define ourselves as we are now, and that how we choose to exercise this freedom is up to each of us.

Getting what we want can put us in a good position to embark on a journey of self-discovery and self-development. It can serve as a springboard to answering, "Where to? What next?"

So, what's next for you? Where are you headed?

***

Rick Eigenbrod, Ph.D.

R ick is an experienced Executive Coach and Organizational Development Consultant whose expertise centers on client growth and performance through innovative approaches to leadership development, change management, and team effectiveness. Projects include the co-design and facilitation of a yearlong leadership development program for the top 250 leaders of an American owned European energy company and also for the executive team and 150 senior managers of a USA multi-media communications corporation.

Previously, Rick was Vice President, Consulting Services of the Right Management Consultants' organizational development practice in Silicon Valley, CA. He provided individual and organizational effectiveness and management consulting services to technology companies throughout the various phases of a company's life cycle.

Rick has an extensive background in organizational development specializing in work with senior management in the areas of Leadership Effectiveness, Executive Team Development & Facilitation, and Organizational Culture. He has managed change management and performance enhancement projects for organizations such as AT&T, Genencor, Life Technologies, Altera Corporation, Carl Zeiss Meditec, Inc., United HealthCare, the Hewlett Foundation and Google.

He has served as Chairman of three groups of CEOs for Vistage International as well as serving for over 20 years as a Resource Speaker for more than 500 Vistage groups nationwide and was USA Speaker of the Year for Vistage Canada. Rick continues to be a featured speaker at Vistage and corporate management meetings throughout the United States and Canada.

Early in his career, Rick was Co-Director of Psychological Services, Counseling Center at the University of California, Davis. He also served as the Training Development Officer for Peace Corps (N25) Nepal. For 10 years he conducted Communication Skills Training for the United States Air Force in the U.S., Europe, and the Far East.

Rick holds a Ph.D., from Michigan State University in Clinical Psychology, a M.A. from Auburn University, and a B.A., from Tulane University. He has been a long standing member of the American Psychological Association.

Connect with Dr. Eigenbrod

eigenbrod@candescencemedia.com

Made in the USA
San Bernardino, CA
07 April 2017